I was like a boy playing on the seashore,
and diverting myself now and then finding a smoother pebble
or a prettier shell than ordinary, while the great ocean
of truth lay all undiscovered before me.
—Isaac Newton

Urania, the Greek muse of the science of astronomy

Lives of the Scientists

Experiments, Explosions
(and What the Neighbors Thought)

WRITTEN BY **Kathleen Krull**

ILLUSTRATED BY **Kathryn Hewitt**

Harcourt Children's Books
Houghton Mifflin Harcourt
Boston New York 2013

Thanks to Jeannette Larson, editor extraordinaire, and to Elizabeth Tardiff, Christine Kettner,
and Adah Nuchi for all their brilliant design and editorial work.
—K.H.

Text copyright © 2013 by Kathleen Krull
Illustrations copyright © 2013 by Kathryn Hewitt

Harcourt Children's Books is an imprint of Houghton Mifflin Harcourt Publishing Company.

www.hmhbooks.com

The illustrations in this book were done in oil paint on Arches paper.
The text type was set in Dante MT.
The display type was set in Youngblood Antique.

Library of Congress Cataloging-in-Publication Data is available.
ISBN 978-0-15-205909-5
LCCN 2012953333

Manufactured in China
SCP 10 9 8 7 6 5 4 3 2 1
4500405808

For my friends Jean Ferris and Sheila Cole

—K.K.

For Arlo, born with infinite curiosity about the

smallest bugs and the biggest stars

—K.H.

Contents

Introduction • 9

Dragons and Frogs
ZHANG HENG • 12

Writing on Horseback
IBN SĪNĀ • 14

Full of Stars—and Himself
GALILEO • 17

The Importance of an Apple
ISAAC NEWTON • 23

"Promise Not to Call Me a Lunatic"
WILLIAM AND CAROLINE HERSCHEL • 29

Throwing Up at the Sight of Blood
CHARLES DARWIN • 35

Caterpillars in the Lab
LOUIS PASTEUR • 41

Very Famous Dogs
IVAN PAVLOV • 46

Science Can Be Delicious
GEORGE WASHINGTON CARVER • 49

A Blue-Green Glow
MARIE CURIE • 55

FOOLING AROUND FOR EIGHT HOURS A DAY
ALBERT EINSTEIN • 61

COWBOY SONGS IN THE DARK
EDWIN HUBBLE • 67

WATERING CORN WITH HER TEARS
BARBARA McCLINTOCK • 73

"COMPUTERS WERE MORE FUN"
GRACE MURRAY HOPPER • 78

IMAGINING SURF
RACHEL CARSON • 81

"A DEAR OLD FRIEND"
CHIEN-SHIUNG WU • 84

"TWO PEOPLE ARE BETTER THAN ONE"
JAMES D. WATSON AND FRANCIS CRICK • 87

FROM WAITRESS TO WORLD EXPERT
JANE GOODALL • 93

FOR FURTHER READING • 96

Lives of the Scientists

~ INTRODUCTION ~

Meet twenty dazzling scientists, some of the superstars who moved science forward. Other books explore the details of their discoveries. This book is about their lives. What were these men and women like as human beings—in the laboratory and out of it? How would their neighbors have viewed them?

All were geniuses in one way or another. Many had prickly personalities. Many blew things up or sneaked into the lab to work in the middle of the night. Many had superb writing skills that shaped their careers. And many took wrong turns in their research and in life—even geniuses make mistakes.

But which one personally attended the hangings of criminals he'd sentenced to death (Newton)? Whose house was stoned by scandalized neighbors (Curie)? Whose noisy stomach ailments prevented him from staying over at other people's houses (Darwin)? Which one chased a student out of his lab (Pavlov), and which one frightened students into slipping out the back door (McClintock)? Who was featured in glamorous *Vogue* magazine (Watson), and who was jealous (Crick)? Who mastered the art of carrying thirteen dinner plates without dropping them (Goodall), and who was asked to be president of a country (Einstein)? Who was constantly being hunted by his enemies (Ibn Sīnā), and who lived out his last years under house arrest (Galileo)? The lives of famous scientists turn out to hold one surprise after another.

Ever since the days when most people believed the world was flat, many have found science to be taxing on the brain. Science is often about things that are invisible or concepts that seem counterintuitive. But from the earliest Chinese and Islamic science to the years after 1901 (when the fortune left by Swedish dynamite inventor Alfred Nobel began to fund the famous Nobel Prizes) to the present day, science is too amazing to ignore.

Here are biographies of twenty men and women, warts and all, the real people behind some of the mind-boggling discoveries that continue to shape our world.

—*Kathleen Krull*

Lives of the Scientists

Zhang Heng

BORN IN NANYANG, CHINA, 78

DIED IN LUOYANG, CHINA, 139

*Astronomer who influenced centuries of
Chinese accomplishments in science*

The imperial court of the mighty Han dynasty teemed with actors, acrobats, wrestlers, pig breeders—and scholars, like the multitalented Zhang Heng, product of a solid Confucian education. The emperor first summoned Zhang for his genius at math, but it could just as easily have been his skill at poetry ("Contemplating the Cosmos"), painting (he was considered one of the best painters of his time), or mapmaking.

At age thirty, Zhang started making discoveries in astronomy and was promoted to chief astronomer. His duties included monitoring the earthquakes that shook China. Devastating quakes were believed to be punishment from the gods for poor government. So besides keeping track of the stars, Zhang kept track of the people in power, which made him quite powerful himself. He wore robes of silk, with duck plumes on his fox coats. He dined well on owl spiced with purple ginger and spring garlic, or mandarin duck with bamboo shoots, lotus roots, and mustard greens.

But Zhang also studied earthquakes from a more scientific angle. He invented the world's first primitive seismometer to indicate where an earthquake was happening. The copper machine had eight dragons around the top, each with a copper ball in its mouth. Below were eight frogs, each representing a direction, like the points of a compass. An earthquake would cause a ball to clatter from a dragon's mouth into a frog's mouth.

One day Zhang's invention showed an earthquake rocking to the northwest. With no tremors felt at court, his enemies were snickering—until a messenger brought news of a quake a few hundred miles northwest of the capital. Zhang's salary jumped from a modest six hundred bushels of grain to two thousand, converted into money or bolts of silk.

Until he died, at age sixty-one, Zhang invented many more clever machines, cataloged the stars (twenty-five hundred in all), and continued to interpret events in the skies as a guide to royal behavior.

WRITING ON HORSEBACK

Ibn Sīnā

BORN IN PRESENT-DAY UZBEKISTAN, 980
DIED ON THE ROAD IN PRESENT-DAY IRAN, 1037

**Known in the West as Avicenna,
star of the Islamic golden age of science**

Neighbors were startled by Ibn Sīnā's brain. A devout Muslim, he memorized the entire Koran by age ten, heeding its message of esteeming knowledge. He set out to master all the known sciences, specializing in medicine, and became a practicing doctor at eighteen.

When an important prince fell seriously ill, it was Ibn Sīnā who was called to court and came to his rescue. The grateful ruler granted him access to the royal library. What a thrill for the young doctor to see rooms of rare science books and to take notes on papyrus cards. The only volume that almost thwarted him was Aristotle's *Metaphysics,* which he tried to read and understand forty times before a bookseller sold him a helpful guide; Ibn Sīnā made a large donation to the poor as thanks.

He became a prized advisor. A handsome man in brocaded robes, a turban of linen, and soft leather boots, he was considered an ornament to any Muslim court.

But his was a time of inescapable tribal and religious warfare, and enemies forced him into a lifestyle more harrowing than the average scientist's. They were always hunting him down, trying to poison him or throw him in jail. A wily survivor, he foiled them by moving from city to city along the fabled trade route known as the

Silk Road. By day he was a doctor and administrator; at night he gathered students for scientific discussion, snacks of almonds or pistachios, and wild parties with wine and dancing.

Perhaps because he claimed to never sleep a night through—and because he learned how to write anywhere, even on horseback—Ibn Sīnā was also a prolific author. He penned as many as fifty pages a day, usually in Arabic, the language of Muslim scholarship, not his native Persian. His 240 surviving works include the famous *Canon of Medicine*. Building on the knowledge of the Ancient Greeks Galen and Hippocrates, he came up with a complete system of medicine. He considered medicine a science, not a craft, nor a matter of magic or evil spirits, as was still the belief in Europe. But his influence spread to Europe and elsewhere, and for the next six hundred years, his book was the last word on medical treatment.

FULL OF STARS—AND HIMSELF
Galileo

BORN IN PISA, ITALY, 1564
DIED NEAR FLORENCE, ITALY, 1642

Italian astronomer known as the Father of Modern Science

With his bushy red hair and full red beard, Galileo cut a dashing figure—never mind that his clothes were years out of fashion. He could talk with wit and insight about anything. He was a good writer, an excellent painter (he became an instructor), and a capable lutist. Before his education at a monastery, young Galileo had been tutored by his father, a well-known musician at a time when music was considered a branch of math. Galileo had excelled, of course, at math and all the science of his day.

It was his ego that kept getting in the way. Those who disagreed with him weren't just wrong, they were idiots—even his mother. It is said that when he called her names, she hauled the boy before the Roman Inquisition, which gave him a scolding.

But Galileo just became more obnoxious as he grew up. In many loud arguments at dinner parties, he honed his skill at wielding insults, calling people mental pygmies, morons "hardly deserving to be called human beings." At one university, he didn't just refuse to wear the academic black toga; he wrote a three-hundred-line poem making fun of it. He taught astrology and prepared horoscopes in the style of the times, but he relished pointing out how predictions tended to become true only after they had happened.

The happiest time of his life was the eighteen years he spent teaching science at the University of Padua. Between his duties, he liked to gamble and party—he praised red wine as "light held together by moisture." As a professor without much income, Galileo was not considered a good catch. But with his girlfriend, Marina Gamba, he had two daughters, whom he placed in a convent at a young age, and one son. (Marina later married someone else.) He kept studying on his own, polishing elegant papers like "Discourse on Bodies That Stay Atop Water or Move Within It." He got by on little sleep and worked for hours in his garden, dressed in an old leather apron, taking care of fruit trees—oranges, lemons, citrons—and his vineyard, where he made his own wine.

After his father died, Galileo supported his extended family, and was shorter of money than ever. In his modest villa in the hills above Florence, he tutored young noblemen in military architecture and fortification. At one point he was housing sixteen students and their seventeen servants; if he fell ill, he had to go to someone else's house to get the rest he needed.

He exchanged hundreds of letters with his older daughter, Sister Maria Celeste, a "woman of exquisite mind." He sent her his laundry to be washed, his manuscripts to be copied, and his special spinach casserole. She sent him candied fruits and ripe plums to eat with his partridge dinners, herbal potions to ward off the plague, and pleas to cut back on the wine.

During an era when most people believed that angels moved the planets, Galileo perked up when he heard about a new invention, an "optick tube" for observing the skies. He set one up in his garden, recording each observation. He figured out how to improve the instrument, producing increasingly powerful telescopes he sold for extra cash.

It was an awkward moment when he discovered the four moons orbiting Jupiter. This finding went against the Ancient Greek Ptolemy, who had held that all heavenly bodies circle the Earth. Galileo still dutifully taught this belief in his classes, even though he privately decided that the recent Polish astronomer Nicholas Copernicus was right: the sun is the center of our universe and the Earth is a planet.

Galileo modified his telescope into a microscope and observed fleas, gnats, and moths. But mostly he watched the skies, boosting his ego with more discoveries confirming that poor Ptolemy was quite wrong.

Galileo finally went public at age sixty-eight with his book *Dialogue Concerning the Two Chief World Systems*. To illustrate the debate between the systems of Ptolemy and Copernicus, he invented a character, Simplicio, to defend Ptolemy, sometimes foolishly. Then Galileo went too far by putting the words of the current pope into the mouth of silly Simplicio.

Pope Urban VIII had admired Galileo's brilliance. No more. Galileo was summoned to Rome, ordered to defend his writings to the cardinals of the Roman Inquisition, and forced to stand trial for holding beliefs opposed to the Church. Knowing this would be a hard trip at his age, he made out his will before he left. But he fully expected that he'd be granted a pardon, saying, "I have committed no crime."

During the trial Galileo stayed mostly in comfortable surroundings. He was not thrown into the dungeon, nor tortured or mistreated. But as he became aware of the risk that this treatment could change at any time, he grew more and more tense. After one session with his ten inquisitors, "the poor man has come back more dead than alive," said his host.

Eventually Galileo panicked, took back his words, and begged for mercy. He claimed his "error" was due to ego, his "vainglorious ambition." His punishment was not bad—he was placed under house arrest for the rest of his life.

Ultimately he lived again in his villa, which he referred to as "my prison." He couldn't ask for more merciful treatment, or he'd have been sent to a real prison.

He was often ill, possibly with gout. It was a painful blow when Maria Celeste died at age thirty-three. Then he went blind, mourning that his world had now shrunk to what he could detect with his other four senses. Ego intact, he called it "this universe, which I, by marvelous discoveries and clear demonstrations, have enlarged a hundred thousand times beyond the belief of the wise men of bygone ages."

He was sometimes heard crying during the night. But he never stopped working, despite his crushing humiliation, and died at age seventy-seven.

EXTRA CREDIT

Galileo's *Dialogue,* though it represented the birth of modern astronomy (he had suspected as much), was banned in Italy for two hundred years. It had to be smuggled out and published in other countries. In 1992 Pope John Paul II issued a formal apology for the Church's treatment of Galileo. Three years later, the American spacecraft *Galileo* reached the planet Jupiter.

Fans preserved parts of Galileo's body. You can see several fingers and a tooth at a science museum in Florence.

Galileo lives on not just in science, but in popular culture—for example, in the song "Galileo" by the Indigo Girls and in the loud repetition of his name during the pop group Queen's song "Bohemian Rhapsody."

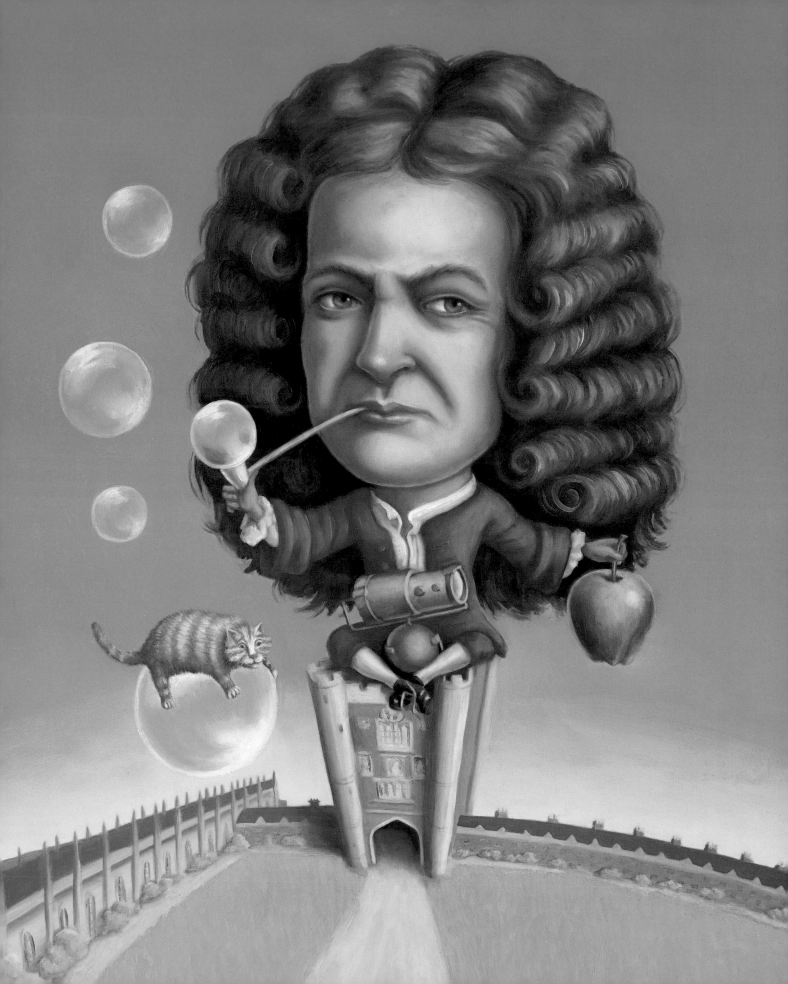

THE IMPORTANCE OF AN APPLE

Isaac Newton

BORN IN LINCOLNSHIRE, ENGLAND, 1642
DIED IN KENSINGTON, ENGLAND, 1727

English scientist who laid the basis for modern physics

For contributing more to the development of science than any other individual in history, Albert Einstein called Isaac Newton the brainiest person ever: "Nature to him was an open book. . . . He stands before us strong, certain, and alone."

"Alone" is the key word. Newton was isolated as a scientist and as a human being. The farmhouse where he grew up in rural England was so hidden that the nearest major road was a mile away. There were no neighbors near the rundown gray house, nor any siblings to play with; there were no books, no clocks, no machines, just a huge orchard of apple trees. The smell of manure was ever present—wool from two hundred sheep was the main family business—and so was dust, when the sheep were being sheared.

His father (who died before Newton was born) was illiterate and couldn't sign his own name, and his mother frowned on education. She was always trying to pull her son out of school to work on the farm, yet he proved he was terrible at farming again and again. When she remarried she moved out, and except for his ancient grandparents, Newton was essentially left on his own for eight years during his early childhood.

But an uncle and the local headmaster sensed a giant brain at work, and made sure school was on Newton's agenda. It took a while, but he rose to the top of his class—though if "plays well with others" had been listed on his report card, he probably would have failed. Even as a child he was fragile, the smallest criticism putting him in a bad mood for months. He mostly kept to himself, and when he did mingle, it was nearly always with girls, who probably didn't give him as hard a time as boys did. Much later, one of the girls remembered holding hands with him. If this is true, it is the first and last mention of a romantic attachment.

Once Newton got to the University of Cambridge, he stayed put for thirty-five years—as a student, then a professor—and it is hard to imagine a quieter life. Even as a student, he seldom took part in campus activities and came off as a bit of a prig. Some who knew him for years reported that they'd heard him laugh only once.

He was a devout member of the Church of England, the state religion, and of the first ten precious books he bought, four were about religion. He threw himself into studies, rarely looking up, taking notes with quill pens. He had a roommate (with whom he didn't get along) but was mostly alone in his airless rooms, telling time by watching the shadows on the wall.

Newton's very first science experiments were wrong turns. He would try to test his vision by pushing his eyeball around inside the socket. He brewed a potion of rose water and turpentine he thought might protect him from the dreaded plague. Somehow he stayed healthy, but eventually the threat of the plague's contagion closed the university and forced him back to his lonely farmhouse, where he plunged into . . . thinking a lot.

Stunning discoveries began mounting up: When an apple fell on his head, he responded with the law of universal gravitation. (Although many assume the apple story is a myth, Newton always insisted it was true.) Then he invented calculus, a new branch of math. He made breakthroughs about colors, light, and rainbows (fixating on red as his favorite color—his drapes and furnishings were always red). He laid all the groundwork for his famous three laws of motion. He was still only twenty-three years old.

But Newton's life had little balance. Deep in thought, he'd stay up all night. He never exercised and had no hobbies, nor any use for music, art, or poetry. His meals were gruel or milk with eggs, perhaps an apple or a bit of roasted quince. But he

often forgot to eat. He reportedly had a cat that became ever larger from eating food off Newton's plate. He couldn't have cared less about his clothes (he slept in them) or combing his hair.

Back at Cambridge, as his discoveries started making him better known, he remained sarcastic and petty, sometimes pouting unattractively. Protective of his isolation, he disliked his growing fame and did nothing to encourage it.

In fact, Newton waited till he was forty-four before he published his masterpiece, *Principia*. He deliberately made the book more difficult than it had to be "to avoid being baited by little smatterers in mathematics." "Smatterers" was his smirking term for amateurs he didn't want to deal with.

Newton wasn't right about everything. He spent a total of thirty years doing experiments in cauldrons in his lab. The focus was alchemy (turning metals into gold, considered a bogus "science" even in his time), and he wrote more about this than actual science.

He was obsessed with biblical prophecy and the idea of the end of the world. He even chose a date (beware: it's the year 2060). None of his work in science ever made Newton question his religious faith: "In the absence of any other proof, the thumb alone would convince me of God's existence."

In a surprising turn of events, Cambridge sent Newton to London to represent the university at Parliament. He seldom spoke during debates, but he came to like London enough to move there. He somehow got appointed to a cushy job in the government: warden of the Royal Mint. Besides a salary, he got a commission on the amount of silver that was minted. Newton had little to do with women, but he must have liked his niece, because she moved in with him, lessening his isolation. He began to give fancy dinner parties and even became a little plump, keeping all his teeth except one. He was finally seen to smile and laugh, though not very often.

Over his last twenty-seven years, he blew soap bubbles and inspected them (to study the interference of light) in the morning, then went to work hunting down criminals who counterfeited money. In one year alone he sent over two dozen counterfeiters to be hanged, and he always attended the executions, though it wasn't a required part of his job.

At age eighty-four, in pain but refusing painkillers, Newton died from various ailments. He couldn't stand his three half siblings, but he left his considerable estate to their children, his eight nieces and nephews.

EXTRA CREDIT

— Newton wrote his *Principia* in Latin, the language of scholars. It came to be considered the first book on modern physics, although due to lack of demand, it was not translated into English until two years after his death.

— Because of Newton's influence, educating children in science became important. In 1761, John Newbery, the English publisher who fostered children's literature (and for whom the Newbery Medal is named), published *The Newtonian System of Philosophy Adapted to the Capacities of Young Gentlemen and Ladies.*

"Promise Not to Call Me a Lunatic"
William and Caroline Herschel

BORN IN HANOVER, GERMANY, 1738;
DIED IN SLOUGH, ENGLAND, 1822 (WILLIAM)
BORN IN 1750 AND DIED IN 1848 IN HANOVER, GERMANY (CAROLINE)

*German-born British astronomer siblings,
considered the parents of astronomy*

"By way of relaxation we talked of astronomy," Caroline Herschel wrote of her new life with her beloved brother William. She was twenty-two, he was thirty-four, and he had just brought her from their hometown in Germany to England.

Caroline was unusually small, less than five feet tall, with unruly curls and smallpox scars. No one believed she would marry. As a girl she had learned the basics of reading and writing and went straight to being treated as the family servant. But she'd been interested in astronomy since their father had taken her "on a clear frosty night into the street, to make me acquainted with several of the beautiful constellations." To leave home, she had to knit enough socks to last the family two years, and William had to promise their mother that he would pay for a real servant.

Caroline never did marry or have children, instead sticking with William. He had left Germany to escape a bloody war and established himself as a musician in Bath, a fashionable English spa town. He played several instruments, composed symphonies (twenty-four in all), taught music, and conducted orchestras. It was while riding his horse between towns to play that he started studying the stars overhead. (If it was daylight, he read books while riding. Once when his horse stumbled, he flew into the air, did a complete somersault, and landed on his feet, book in hand.)

As he took Caroline to his house upon her arrival in England, he had her sit atop the carriage so he could point out the stars. Astronomy was increasingly his obsession; he had started his first astronomical observations journal, and his music had become the way to finance his science. He was only an amateur scientist, this "musician of Bath," but he was determined to make his mark. He had little formal education and Caroline had less, but she was going to be his secret weapon.

His methods were a cross between nurturing and bullying. On his sister's second day in her new country, William started instructing her in English, math, and bookkeeping, with three singing lessons a day. He filled her in on astronomy, constantly plotting how he could get better telescopes to make more accurate observations of the skies.

Within five years Caroline was singing solos in public (turning down work unless William was the conductor) and devoting every clear night to helping her broth-

er. She kept him supplied with coffee and recorded the observations he yelled to her from the elevated platform he'd built. Even when temperatures plunged, her ink freezing in its inkwell, they simply put on more layers of clothes and kept working. Exhausted after long nights, both would sleep in until midday.

Their house turned into a workshop for making better telescopes. William had to polish each telescopic mirror by hand, a process that took hours, while Caroline fed him bits of food and drink. All the while the smell of horse poop (used to make the molds for the mirrors) filled the air.

It was messy work. They didn't always take the time to change out of their good clothes before they built telescopes, and Caroline mourned that "many a lace ruffle . . . was torn or bespattered by molten pitch." Once, while sharpening a tool, William ripped off one of his fingernails. Then one night Caroline's leg got impaled on an iron hook. "I am hooked!" she kept screaming, but William couldn't hear her from high on his observation platform. When she was finally rescued, a chunk of her skin was left behind.

She took two days off from work but never complained. She had become indispensable to their goal of cataloging every object they saw and was starting to spot things he missed. She was the observer during his absences and did all his calculations. (Having learned her multiplication tables so late in life, she never really conquered them and had to carry a cheat sheet in her pocket.)

Neither was particularly religious. Neighbors feared their eccentricities—and were appalled when William cut down any tree that blocked the sky—but others admired his telescopes. He sold sixty of them around the world at a good profit. His masterpiece was a forty-foot-long tube with a four-foot mirror. When it was done, the Herschels threw a party with music, everyone dancing in and out of the tube, Caroline being the nimblest.

One night in 1781, William noticed an object that he assumed was a comet. But it wasn't acting very comet-like, and it turned out to be the first planet to be discovered since prehistoric times. Elated, William tried to name it after King George III.

Others tried to name it Herschel. The name that stuck was Uranus, in honor of both the god of the sky in Greek myth and Urania, the goddess of astronomy.

The discovery made him famous: "I have looked further into space than ever a human being did before me." He was offered the job of personal astronomer to the king, and though it was a big drop in income, it meant he could finally be a full-time scientist. Both Herschels promptly gave up music. The fun part of the royal job was putting on nighttime demonstrations of the stars for the three teenage princesses. But the hard work continued afterward, long into the evening.

In her "Book of Work Done," Caroline began noting her own discoveries. She identified three nebulae, followed by a comet—known as "the first lady's comet." She started earning a salary from the king as well. She was the first woman to get paid for her work in science (at a time when few men did either), and it was the first money she'd ever had to spend for herself.

Then William rather abruptly married a neighbor, a wealthy widow. The new wife insisted that Caroline move out of the house, and William seems to have done little to lessen his sister's resentment of this treatment after their sixteen years of working together. Caroline discovered her second comet a month after the wedding, followed by six more. But in her private diary—where she scribbled prickly thoughts about those she considered idiots and gossips—she apparently expressed her humiliation. The relationship between the women eventually improved, and Caroline destroyed every page she'd written about the conflict.

William died at age eighty-three, but Caroline powered on. She completed the cataloging of twenty-five hundred nebulae and many star clusters. She also nurtured John, William's only son, guiding his education. John said of his aunt at age eighty-three, "She runs about the town with me, and skips up her two flights of stairs . . . sings old rhymes, nay, even dances."

Caroline continued to receive the admiration of all who knew her, and died at age ninety-seven.

EXTRA CREDIT

William poured energy into trying to prove that every planet was inhabited. His first paper to England's Royal Society ("Promise not to call me a lunatic," he begged) proposed that the moon's craters were actually cities built by "Lunarians" to harness the power of the sun. Proof of life on other planets has yet to be found.

John Herschel became a famous scientist in his own right, with discoveries in many fields, making the Herschels one of science's all-time distinguished families.

Throwing Up at the Sight of Blood

Charles Darwin

Born in Shrewsbury, England, 1809
Died in Kent, England, 1882

English biologist who provided the foundation for modern biology

Science was not always considered a scholarly subject. In England in the nineteenth century, it was a fine hobby for gentlemen, on a par with riding horses and hunting. And Charles Darwin was a gentleman—loving brother, obedient son, devoted husband and father, strongly antiracist and antislavery. Other than inhaling snuff, not drawing well, having no ear for music, and being bored by Shakespeare, he had no major faults.

One day, his father, a successful doctor who invested his money wisely, gave his young son two precious natural history books. Darwin became obsessed with nature, beetles in particular. One time he had a different rare beetle in each hand, so when he spied a third beetle, his only way to carry it was to pop it in his mouth—he learned that he didn't care for the taste. His first love, a neighbor named Fanny, married someone else; in her letters to Darwin, she seemed to resent the amount of attention he'd paid to beetles.

Technically Darwin was wealthy enough not to work, but he tried to become a respectable doctor like his dad. There was just that small problem of throwing up at the sight of blood. (Later, his children learned he was not the parent to go to when they were bleeding.) Then he tried to become an Anglican parson, though he didn't go along with all the doctrines of the Church of England. Neither career path worked out.

Instead, his whole life was shaped by the rousing "Yes" he gave at age twenty-two: Would he be willing to work as an unpaid "gentleman naturalist" on the HMS *Beagle*? This navy ship would map the coast of South America—including the mysterious Galápagos Islands with their giant tortoises and creatures seen nowhere else—and would sail on to the Pacific Islands and Australia, ultimately circling the world.

Once aboard the ship, gung ho as he was, Darwin was unprepared for his constant vomiting due to seasickness. He sustained himself with raisins and tried to keep down lemon juice to head off scurvy. Still, he was experiencing nature in a way few people had, and it was heaven: "The mind is a chaos of delight." Besides keeping the captain company at dinner, Darwin's job was to observe. He threw himself into collecting samples of every plant and fossil, writing notes like mad, and reading books by Charles Lyell about the new science of geology, the study of how Earth has evolved.

Five years later, Darwin was actually a bit relieved to be back in England, along with two tortoises he had brought home as pets. He retreated to his study to analyze his observations, and he started having frequent stomach pains. He had a lot of new

ideas, but he knew no one who was ready for them; his extensive notebooks represented his whole secret life.

He did venture out to the London Zoo, mainly to observe the latest sensations: an orangutan and a chimpanzee. No one in England had seen these animals before, and everyone—including Darwin—was shocked by how closely they resembled humans.

At age twenty-nine he married his cousin Emma, after calling on her a few times and jotting on paper that a wife would be "better than a dog anyhow." He welcomed their children into his study to inspect jars of insects, and he encouraged their contributions to his experiments with plants. Only seven of their ten children survived past childhood; he was especially close to his oldest daughter, and her death broke his heart.

On his country estate, full of worms and other natural wonders, Darwin took daily walks with his dog Polly, thinking endlessly. He wrote lots of letters to various experts—fourteen thousand letters to and from him survive—amassing a mountain of evidence for his ideas on everything from honeybees, cave fish, algae, pigeons, barnacles, and berries to creatures he'd seen in the Galápagos and to his beloved beetles.

Years passed. Darwin's stomach problems worsened, even on a bland diet of

bananas. He could never get warm, despite wearing wool underwear and keeping a fire going year-round. Extreme flatulence kept him from staying at other people's houses. No one has ever pinned down what was wrong with Darwin medically, but the only thing that seemed to help was taking the icy-cold "water cure" at a spa. Even there he couldn't leave work behind, following ants around to trace their journeys. Once he paid a stranger to follow a second ant going in the opposite direction; a carriage passed by, full of onlookers giggling at the sight of two men creeping along, watching the ground.

The main problem with Darwin's health may have been his dread at publishing his theories, realizing that they didn't always fit with a literal interpretation of the Bible. Darwin saw no conflict between science and religion, but he knew many who did—including his own wife.

Finally, at age fifty, he knew others were about to beat him at publishing his own ideas. So he revved himself up and published *On the Origin of Species by Means of Natural Selection,* all about evolution. He wasn't inventing the idea of evolution—people were already talking about it. Darwin was proposing a method for how it worked ("It is not the strongest of the species that survive, nor the most intelligent, but the ones most responsive to change") and asserting that change in nature was nonstop. He predicted that "intermediate forms," or missing links, would be discovered that would confirm his theory.

While writing, he took breaks only for spas, vomiting, playing pool, and, at night, losing backgammon games to Emma or listening to her play piano.

Before Darwin, "Because . . ." was a legitimate answer to why plants and animals were the way they were. But Darwin offered a theory, a hypothesis that could be tested, a new framework in which scientists could examine our world.

But non-scientists found his book humiliating, even enraging, perhaps illegal. How dare he challenge ideas that had stood *unchallenged* for centuries? Some (though not all) from the Church of England loudly objected. And so began the ongoing screaming debate over Darwin's theory of evolution.

He backed off, letting others carry on the fray, his ever-growing beard protecting him from the world. He spent his last twenty years investigating his favorite things—mold, Venus flytraps, human faces, worms, orchids. He doted on his grandson Bernard, who called him Baba, and let him draw pictures on his study floor while he worked.

Darwin's health never did improve, with bad days and less-than-bad days. He would write, "But I am very poorly today and very stupid and hate everybody and everything. One lives only to make blunders." Despite all his complaints, he lasted until age seventy-three, when he died of heart failure.

EXTRA CREDIT

∼ *On the Origin of Species* became one of the most influential books ever published. Darwin's theory of evolution became accepted by the scientific community and much of the public as the years went on, and today's biology as well as other sciences are based on it.

∼ In September 2008, the Church of England officially apologized to Darwin "for misunderstanding you and, by getting our first reaction wrong, encouraging others to misunderstand you still."

∼ Discoveries about Darwin's missing links have mounted up over the years, most famously in 1974 with a fossilized creature scientists named Lucy. Showing traits of humans as well as apes, it was believed to be 3.2 million years old.

CATERPILLARS IN THE LAB

Louis Pasteur

BORN IN DOLE, FRANCE, 1822
DIED IN SAINT-CLOUD, FRANCE, 1895

French chemist and microbiologist who revolutionized medicine

"Please keep in mind that I have never even touched a silkworm," Louis Pasteur argued when he first got the request.

The lucrative silkworm industry (every farm in France was partly devoted to it) was going under because the caterpillars were dying mysteriously instead of producing silk. Pasteur, a star professor of chemistry, was asked to help, but he knew virtually nothing about these wiggly worms. Still, super-patriotic, he devoted the next six years of his life to them. Becoming an expert breeder, he finally identified an organism infecting the caterpillars—and saved the French silk business. A triumph for him, it was a leap ahead in learning about infectious diseases.

Pasteur had started out as an average student, more gifted in painting portraits than anything, taking lessons in singing and glass blowing. But at age seventeen, he wrote that "in science, one is happy." He hated math but loved chemistry so much that he got to classes half an hour early to get a good seat. The first experiment he carried out in class, producing natural phosphorus with its yellow glow, tickled him no end.

At age twenty-six, Pasteur joined the faculty at the University of Strasbourg and was determined to wed Marie, the daughter of the university's rector. He wrote a letter to Marie's father asking for her hand, also mentioning his love of science for its own sake. The courtship consisted of his asking her the exact times she'd be home, so he wouldn't be wasting his valuable time waiting for her. His letters to her got mushier: he acknowledged his "cold, shy exterior," but said, "You are everything to me," signing off with "My love to you and to science forever."

Later, Marie's son-in-law said that in thirty years of knowing her, he had never heard her start a sentence with the word "I." She kept the mundane side of daily life away from Pasteur, slipping money into his pocket each morning so he'd have some. A bit of a tyrant, he wrote memos spelling out which buttons needed sewing: "Oh! Wives! How little you know about your husbands' comforts!" Three of their five children died in childhood from typhoid fever, driving Pasteur to focus on finding cures for diseases: "The object of scientific research is the improvement of human health."

Taking a few days off was an unfamiliar sensation to Pasteur: "I did what everybody does. I bathed in the sea. This feels much better than I had thought." His social life was minimal, though he did like to play croquet and pool and had a philosopher friend who was able to distract him. At night he dictated his research papers to Marie. Sometimes his son's jokes made him laugh, but mostly Pasteur's family became used to him pacing a room in silence. He slept only two to three hours a night and preferred simple, frugal meals. Raised Catholic, Pasteur remained devout, believing that science and religion had nothing to do with each other. He became a bit germaphobic; he would examine a slice of bread for mold before eating it, and he didn't like to shake hands.

By age thirty-two he was an important professor of chemistry and dean of the science faculty at the University of Lille. As a teacher and administrator he was rigid, obsessed with punctuality, without any sense of humor, and unpopular. Students once staged a revolt, refusing to eat some horrible mutton stew (made from the meat of sheep) in the cafeteria. Furious, Pasteur responded by making sure mutton stew was served every single Monday. In the lab he imposed inflexible military discipline;

labs were to him "sacred places." He could be rude and harsh with those who contradicted him.

Pasteur spent untold hours glued to the microscope. In a famous explanation for his successes, he lectured, "Chance favors only the prepared mind." Marie apparently felt neglected: "I make her feel better by telling her that I am leading her into prosperity."

With wine and beer considered safer to drink than water, proper fermentation of alcohol was a serious issue in France. When contamination struck, the emperor himself sought the help of his smartest subjects, such as Pasteur. Pasteur bought a vineyard to use as his personal lab (and even did wine tastings, but strictly for scientific reasons). His research showed that contamination was caused by microbes, and to prevent it, he sterilized the wine by heating it to a specified temperature. He had just invented "pasteurization," a process we still use for milk and other beverages (though not for fine wines, as it kills the organisms that contribute to the aging process).

Then came six years with the caterpillars and further triumphs—"The life of a scientist is so short!" Around Europe, an anthrax epidemic was killing many sheep and some people as well. When Pasteur supplied evidence that the anthrax bacillus was causing the infection, this pointed to the new germ theory of disease, the main concept underlying modern medicine.

After developing a vaccine against anthrax, Pasteur moved on to rabies, a much-dreaded disease. At age sixty-two, he vaccinated a nine-year-old boy who had been bitten by a rabid dog, and was treated as a hero for saving his life. He went on to save many more, using the vaccine to prevent the disease in the first place. This was the birth of preventive medicine. Now an international legend, a scientific superhero, he had no trouble raising funds to build the Pasteur Institute, a foundation devoted to curing infectious diseases. There the walls were decorated with portraits and pastels from Pasteur's early days as an artist.

When he was partially paralyzed after a stroke, doctors treated Pasteur by applying leeches behind his ears. He limped into his seventieth birthday party, which teemed with worshipful fellow scientists. His paralysis worsened, and he died two years later.

EXTRA CREDIT

Although Pasteur's recommendation that hospitals boil their surgical tools to sterilize them went ignored until the twentieth century, his work furthered huge advances in medical research. After him, more patients left a hospital alive than dead—a tremendous step forward.

For his rescue of the beer, wine, and silk industries in France, plus numerous other accomplishments, almost every French town has a street named after Pasteur, not to mention hospitals and schools.

Ivan Pavlov

BORN IN RYAZAN, RUSSIA, 1849
DIED IN SAINT PETERSBURG, RUSSIA, 1936

*Russian physiologist who won the 1904 Nobel Prize
for research on dogs*

Until his big break, Ivan Pavlov's life was going nowhere. His father had never really forgiven him for not being the seventh-generation Pavlov to become a priest in the Eastern Orthodox Church. Even with his medical degree and superior surgical skill (he could operate with either hand), Pavlov was so poor that he had to live with his brother while his wife, Seraphima, lived with her family.

Not until he was forty-one did he get his dream job as a professor at the new Russian Imperial Medical Academy. He could finally live with his wife, a former teacher, and raise their four scientifically talented children. Pavlov had his own lab, where he experimented with various animals and specialized in the gastric function of dogs. He hated cats ("impatient, loud, malicious"), rabbits were too frail, and pigs were too excitable.

In thousands of experiments on hundreds of canines, Pavlov discovered that if he made a sound, like ringing a bell, when the dogs were fed, they would start salivating at the sound whether or not food was present. It was a "conditioned reflex," and Pavlov was the first to describe a concept that became crucial to the study of human psychology. Acting like "Pavlov's dogs" came to refer to an instinctive, unthinking reaction to a situation.

Some made fun of his "spitting science," but the Russian government loved him and gave him more labs.

Pavlov genuinely loved dogs and couldn't stand it when one was hurt or died: "But I endure this in the interest of truth, for the benefit of humanity." He gave them names like Cute Little Thing, Buddy, Nice Girl, Old Russian Clown, and Little Friend (his favorite).

Less pleasant with his staff of one hundred, he was insistent on being right, at least once chasing a dissenter out of the lab. He considered his time so valuable that he sometimes told people he could meet with them only during his walks between labs, and many (including his wife) couldn't keep up. Aware of his penchant for punctuality, friends who arrived a minute early would stand outside his door, waiting until the precise moment to knock.

In his office Pavlov would serve sweet tea, Ukrainian bacon, and black bread. Outside the office, he helped finance his lavish lab by marketing canine gastric fluid. He claimed that a glass of it would enable very ill people to eat, and was eventually selling fifteen thousand containers of "appetite juice" a year.

He loved "muscular joy"—he went cross-country skiing, started a gymnastics club, excelled at the Russian game of gorodki, with its heavy wooden pins—and lasted until age eighty-six.

Science Can Be Delicious

George Washington Carver

Born near Diamond Grove, Missouri, 1864(?)
Died in Tuskegee, Alabama, 1943

African American botanist

Few have had more barriers to a science career than George Washington Carver. He was born to slaves owned by Moses Carver, just as slavery was being abolished in America. His father died in an accident before his birth, and then baby George and his mother were kidnapped by slave raiders. The baby was returned to the plantation, but his mother disappeared.

Carver grew up during a time when everything, from bathrooms to colleges, was strictly and legally divided into "colored" and "white." All his life Carver faced insults and threats, and he was forever haunted after witnessing the lynching of a black man. White friends who traveled with him were shocked to see how often he was refused service in restaurants and hotels, and thus how much planning it took for blacks to travel. Unfailingly considerate, Carver would be more embarrassed for his friends than himself in these situations.

But he was helped by many, black and white, starting with the Moses Carver family, who raised him after he was orphaned. Never physically strong, he was excused from heavy chores at the plantation and allowed to explore. He started a rock collection, a pet frog collection, and a flower garden away from the house. Though he feared being mocked for wasting time, he spent more and more hours in the woods examining nature: "Nothing is more beautiful than the loveliness of the woods before sunrise." He loved to experiment with soil and to discover what conditions were best for each plant. Neighboring farmers came to know him as someone who could save plants from dying and called him the Plant Doctor.

Though he always had a close relationship with the Carvers, he left home at age ten or twelve. He lived at first with the nearest town's midwife and healer in exchange for chores, then moved on in search of schools that would allow blacks to study, working at odd jobs to pay his way. Later, he was the only black at several of the colleges he attended, and his acceptance by students "made me believe I was a real human being." He performed in plays and studied music and art, but he was keenest about the newest science-based techniques of agriculture. His joy was experimenting with plants, cross-fertilizing to see what he could grow; he collected a thousand specimens of fungus.

As the only African American with a graduate degree in agriculture, he was hired as director of agricultural research at what is now Tuskegee University, a historically black college headed by the famous educator Booker T. Washington. Carver

spent forty-seven years there—most of his life. Washington fostered his career more than anyone else, complaining only about Carver's poor skills with paperwork and administration. Carver's job description was so broad that it included making sure the toilets were working, overseeing the grounds, keeping all the livestock fed, and much more. But it also involved research, though at first his lab equipment consisted of pots and pans, teacups, hubcaps, and a microscope he'd been given. It included teaching as well. He liked to amaze students by correctly identifying whatever specimen they brought him. Once some boys tried to trick him by building an insect from parts of other insects—Carver took one look and labeled it a "humbug."

In his travels, Carver was horrified by the poverty of those in the post–Civil War South. Many lived on a cheap diet of molasses and lard, suffering diseases caused by lack of vitamins. Carver began writing nifty little booklets like *How to Grow the Tomato and 115 Ways to Prepare It for the Table.* In all, he wrote more than forty publications about planting such nutritious crops as peanuts, soybeans, and sweet potatoes. To get people excited about these humble foods, he created recipes—he came up with fourteen kinds of candy from the sweet potato alone. Contrary to myth, he did

not invent peanut butter, but he made it tastier with what he called his "cookstove chemistry." Through his efforts, Carver permanently changed southern agriculture for the better.

"In dirt is life" was Carver's motto. He believed anything could be made out of plants, from clothes and cosmetics to alternative fuels, cars, and houses. In his ever-growing lab, he personally developed three hundred products derived from peanuts, and one hundred eighteen from sweet potatoes. He anticipated more plant-based products to follow: "I am not a finisher. I am a blazer of trails." He rarely patented his discoveries, wanting everyone to have free access to them.

With an unusually high voice, Carver was quiet and soft-spoken unless he was using his mighty persuasive skill to speak about his discoveries. He once came close to marrying, but he decided his goals were too different from the woman's, and never considered marriage again. His hands were always moving—tending or painting pictures of plants, writing poetry, playing piano or guitar, doing massage. He made his own clothes and wore them until they almost fell apart, always with a flower or a twig or some berries pinned to his lapel. Deeply religious, he referred to his lab as "God's Little Workshop" and taught Bible classes at his African Methodist Episcopal church.

Carver had an artist's eye for color. During World War II he worked to replace the textile dyes formerly imported from Europe, and in all he produced dyes of five hundred different shades.

Despite a generous salary, Carver had little use for money and spent it on himself only when he needed medical or dental care. He loaned money to students constantly, and when he died he left all of his considerable savings to fund the lab. He used his fame to encourage black students to pursue careers in science, urging them not to focus on their hardships or their life in a hostile world, but on finding ways to make original contributions in areas where "there is no color line; simply the survival of the fittest."

Carver became the most well-known living African American in the world. He met with three American presidents: Theodore Roosevelt, Calvin Coolidge, and

Franklin Roosevelt. Inventor Thomas A. Edison offered him a job with a salary of more than $100,000 a year (he declined). His famous friends included Indian freedom fighter Mohandas Gandhi and car manufacturer Henry Ford, who called him "the world's greatest living scientist" and installed an elevator so he didn't have to climb stairs at Tuskegee. When he died, in his seventies after a bad fall, President Roosevelt stated, "The world of science has lost one of its most eminent figures."

Carver always believed that every school should have a garden, but not necessarily to train students to be farmers or scientists. Nature study, he said, has the "tendency to make the child think, and that is what we are trying to teach him—to think."

EXTRA CREDIT

After Carver's death, the George Washington Carver National Monument was founded at his birthplace. It was the first national park site to honor the life of a black American and a non-president.

There were unproven rumors during his life that Carver was homosexual, and today he is often included in books about famous gay heroes.

Carver is considered a forerunner of today's ecologists and biochemical engineers, careers that technically didn't exist until years later.

Marie Curie

BORN IN WARSAW, POLAND, 1867
DIED IN HAUTE-SAVOIE, FRANCE, 1934

Polish-French chemist and physicist, winner of two Nobel Prizes

"Be less curious about people and more curious about ideas," warned the woman who might have thrown this book out the window. She was so repelled by fame that she sometimes denied being Marie Curie. When people recognized her, she would insist, "You must be mistaken."

To counter the many obstacles she would face as a woman in science, Curie got off to a strong start. Life for her family, in a part of Poland that had been taken over by Russia, was hard, but Curie's mother made sure all five of her children got a solid education. Although many girls were not educated at the time, it never seemed to have occurred to Curie's father to discourage his daughters. Her sister and brother, who wanted to be doctors, were her role models.

But education ended for girls in Poland at age sixteen. Very few Polish women had enough schooling to be admitted to universities elsewhere. For a while Curie attended a highly illegal school called the Flying University, in which women held classes in secret places to escape the notice of Russian police. Then she studied on her own while working as a governess.

Curie, later famous for her patience, finally got herself to the Sorbonne (the University of Paris) at age twenty-four. She adored her classes and excelled in them,

but was often alone. She lived in poverty—no heat, no hot water, little more than chocolate and bread for dinner. Her goal was to return to her family in Poland and use her two science degrees to help her country.

Then she met Pierre, another scientist and the head of a new lab, already known for his work on crystals. He was French, not the Polish patriot she would have liked. But they had too much in common not to marry. Neither was religious, and they had the simplest possible wedding at the town hall. He got her a lab of her own at his school, and would pat her fondly whenever they passed each other. At night they discussed the recent discovery of x-rays and the latest news: the mysterious rays being emitted from uranium.

Pierre refused to consider that Marie give up her research on uranium after marriage, nor after the birth of their two daughters, Irène and Ève. (His father and a nanny helped with child care.) In fact, Pierre soon realized that her work was leading in a more fruitful direction than his, so he joined forces with her.

They lived frugally, had lunches of sausage and tea, and were always on the verge of running out of money. Their one luxury was fresh flowers in every room. In the lab, Marie wore simple dresses in black or navy blue so they wouldn't show stains, and kept wearing them until they got holes.

Within the same year, Marie proposed two new radioactive elements in nature: polonium (named for her beloved Poland) and, even more important, an element she named radium for its intense radioactivity. To pave the way for further discoveries about the structure of the atom, she needed a physical sample of radium. This meant crystallizing substances over and over to get its purest form. It took her four years to produce what she needed, a piece the size of a grain of rice. She worked so hard she lost fifteen pounds: "I would be broken with fatigue at the day's end."

After dinner at night Marie and Pierre would walk back to the lab, spellbound by the blue-green glow of their test tubes, which were "like faint fairy light." Though they were already experiencing such symptoms as constant burning in their fingers, neither worried about exposure to radioactivity; the dangers weren't going to be known for years.

After they won the 1903 Nobel Prize in Physics, the Curies were instantly famous and a bit more financially secure. They were able to hire an assistant in the lab, and at home they installed a modern bathroom and stocked up on caviar.

But reporters were pests, eager for gossipy details, invading their daughters' privacy, wanting to know if Marie also did "womanly" things like cooking. She had little patience for fame. Never good at small talk, she often struck others as cold and reserved; many were simply unused to such a serious woman, so brainy and single-minded. When asked how she could have a family and a scientific career, she said, "Well, it has not been easy." Still, family kept seeing her through. Pierre treated her as the genius she was, and her daughters looked up to her as their hero.

After Pierre was run over by a carriage and instantly killed at age forty-six—possibly because his legs had started weakening due to radiation exposure—Marie almost collapsed. At thirty-eight, she had lost her best friend and her only real peer:

"I will never be able to laugh genuinely until the end of my days." Her way of dealing with grief was to work harder and refuse to allow her husband's name to be spoken, even around her daughters.

She did, however, fall for a former student of Pierre's and a longtime friend of the family, a married father of four. When her love letters were leaked to the press, the scandal was humiliating. Disapproving neighbors stoned her house; a colleague labeled her "a detestable idiot." Young Albert Einstein, whose career she'd been encouraging, gave her advice for handling the embarrassment, though behind her back he was condescending: "She is not attractive enough to represent a danger to anyone."

Winning her second Nobel Prize, for chemistry, was a distraction, and then World War I broke out. Loyal to her adopted country of France, she invented a portable x-ray machine that was installed on military trucks, saving the lives of countless soldiers and introducing American army doctors to x-ray technology.

Curie went on to found the Radium Institute, a world-class research center, and to nurture Irène in one of the great parent-child relationships in science. Irène fulfilled her mother's dream and became the second woman in history to win the Nobel Prize in Chemistry.

Curie's relationship with Ève, who was more interested in music than science, was rockier. Marie disapproved of certain outfits and shoes: "You'll never make me believe women were meant to walk on stilts!" Still, Ève went on to write an inspirational biography of her mother.

Curie wore the same dress to both Nobel ceremonies and throughout her American fund-raising tour, where she was hailed as "the Greatest Woman in the World." She still lived mostly in the lab, but also went hiking in the Alps, liked to swim, and bought several homes.

Surrounded by family, her bones damaged by radiation, Curie died at age sixty-six, having lit a glowing path for countless women to follow.

EXTRA CREDIT

⌐ The first type of radium therapy, called curietherapy, showed promise in cancer treatment. Today radiation is used in about half of cancer cases as one of the weapons for killing cancerous cells.

⌐ Curie considered herself part of a tradition of "guinea pigs"—scientists who don't mind experimenting on themselves to benefit their work. When her office was turned into a museum after her death, the furniture was so radioactive that it was replaced with replicas. For many years, anyone who wanted to touch her contaminated notebooks had to sign a medical release.

⌐ When inhaled or ingested, polonium was found to be one of the most toxic substances in the world. American officials have since put it on the list of the ten most dangerous ingredients that could be used in a terrorist weapon.

Albert Einstein

BORN IN ULM, GERMANY, 1879
DIED IN PRINCETON, NEW JERSEY, 1955

*German-American physicist who changed
ideas about time, matter, and space*

Albert Einstein adored the music of Mozart—so much that when
he heard it coming from a nearby house, he barged in with his trusty violin to play
along, even though he hadn't even met his neighbors yet. Reports differ about his tal-
ent, but no one questioned his passion: "Mozart's music is so pure and beautiful that
I see it as a reflection of the inner beauty of the universe itself," Einstein said. Mozart
helped him see solutions to problems—problems on the largest possible scale.

He grew up surrounded by electricity—the Einstein family business was sup-
plying it—and something as simple as a compass led to his lifelong sense of wonder
about invisible forces. Contrary to myth, young Albert never failed math, and he got
decent grades. But teachers found him irritating, with his know-it-all grin. His first
love might have been irritated, too, when he sent her bags of his dirty clothes to be
washed.

A high school dropout, largely self-educated, Einstein made it into a technical
college, where he fell hard for super-smart Mileva Marić, the only woman in his physics degree program. They took hikes, rode bikes, and talked nonstop about the latest
in theoretical physics.

With his degree, he aimed to teach. But for nine years no university would hire him, thanks mostly to the lack of a good word from his professors. He kept studying independently and published his first paper, which turned out to be all wrong. While he struggled to find work, Mileva had a baby girl she apparently gave up for adoption; her existence was a secret for many years.

When a friend helped him snag a government job, Einstein spent seven years as a clerk in the Swiss patent office, analyzing applications for patents. That may seem like a weird turn for this giant brain, but it meant job security, marriage—and continuing his studies. He could finish his duties in a few hours, then do his own work. He didn't need a lab, because he didn't do traditional experiments; he did what he called "thought experiments," coming up with theories for others to prove. If bosses walked by, he could stuff his science notes into a drawer and pretend to be examining patent applications. At night, he exchanged ideas with other scholars, pulling out his violin to cap off the evening with some Mozart.

After the birth of their two sons, Hans and Eduard, Mileva seemed to give up on being a scientist herself, and Einstein stopped encouraging her. She was his intellectual peer and better at math than he was, but more and more her role seemed to be to serve food, not contribute scientific ideas.

For all his brilliance, Einstein was bad at many things. Family life: "I have *not* bestowed the same care to understanding people as to understanding science," he once said. Wearing socks: He didn't, as he found it annoying when his big toe poked a hole in them. Working in a lab: Once he set off an explosion that almost blew off his hand, leaving him unable to play the violin for weeks. Writing light verse: He did it all his life, not caring that it wasn't as good as his science. Fixing meals: When he remembered to eat at all, he would throw anything into a saucepan. He never learned to drive and had trouble operating simple machines like can openers. And he couldn't swim, but he would go sailing alone without a life jacket, writing notes as the boat drifted.

But somehow in 1905, at age twenty-six, still a clerk, he published four papers that changed science. Each focused on a different aspect of physics, and the most famous laid out his theory of relativity, all about space and time. It was mind-bendingly complex, with its equation $E = mc^2$. The best he could do to simplify it was to say, "Put your hand on a hot stove for a minute, and it seems like a hour. Sit with a pretty girl for an hour, and it seems like a minute. That's relativity."

He later tried to rationalize his "miracle year": "Besides eight hours of work, each day also has eight hours for fooling around, and then there's also Sunday." Finally, at age thirty, he became a junior professor, with more recognition to come. The more successful he became, the more his relationship with Mileva fell apart, with

arguments about the children (Eduard was showing signs of mental illness) and money. He tried treating her like an employee—"I will receive my three meals regularly *in my room*"—and he began an affair with Elsa Einstein, his cousin.

An early present from Elsa—a hairbrush—was a hint to do something about his wild hair. (It didn't work.) He called her "no mental brainstorm," but when they married, she took control of their life in Berlin. He started off each day with a bubble bath and two fried eggs. For lunch she made his favorite foods—salmon with mayonnaise; asparagus; strawberries with whipped cream; pots of black tea and strong coffee.

Einstein's Nobel Prize in Physics in 1922 was a welcome reward, though the prize money went to Mileva to care for Eduard, who was eventually diagnosed with schizophrenia and institutionalized for the rest of his life. Being world-famous was unnerving, but Einstein reacted with a sense of humor, sticking his tongue out for the camera, playing his violin instead of giving a speech, making clever quips. "I am no Einstein," he once said apologetically when he couldn't answer a question.

He would hike for days in the Alps, sometimes with his friend Marie Curie and her daughters. He liked a good joke—his contagious laugh sounded like a squealing seal—and collected such books as *The Hundred Best Jewish Jokes*. A passionate pacifist, he was sometimes politically naive; he believed for a while that Adolf Hitler posed no threat.

At age fifty-four Einstein fled Nazi Germany and settled in a special haven for scholars at Princeton University. He had mixed feelings about America ("Everything—even lunacy—is mass-produced here") but spent his final twenty years in New Jersey with Elsa and numerous pets in a simple white house. Neighbors loved living next door to a genius, famous around town for sleeping nude (which he freely admitted) and playing his violin.

Though not a devout Jew—he rebelled against organized religion—Einstein declared that "science without religion is lame; religion without science is blind." He raised funds for Jewish refugees and personally helped as many as he could. But he said, "I lack both the natural aptitude and the experience to deal properly with people," when he was invited to be president of the then-new country of Israel.

After a blood vessel burst in his stomach, Einstein died at age seventy-six, surrounded by pages of equations.

EXTRA CREDIT

⌁ After Einstein died, his brain was removed by a doctor who put it in a Mason jar, wanting to study it. For forty-three years, he took the jar with him on his random travels all around the country and would send small pieces of the brain to any researcher who asked. He finally dropped what was left back at the Princeton hospital in 1998; it was donated in 2011 to the Mütter Museum in Philadelphia.

⌁ The Baby Einstein Company, with products designed to foster intelligence in young children, pays the Einstein estate so much in royalties that he is one of the highest-earning dead celebrities.

⌁ Evidence continues to verify Einstein's predictions, with thousands of scientists working on the Hubble Space Telescope, the Large Hadron Collider, and other projects influenced by his discoveries.

Cowboy Songs in the Dark

Edwin Hubble

Born in Marshfield, Missouri, 1889
Died in San Marino, California, 1953

*American astronomer who discovered
major new evidence about our universe*

Always very buff, as handsome as a movie star, Edwin Hubble cut a glamorous figure around the American Midwest. In high school he set the state record for the high jump, excelled at basketball, and was such a good boxer that fight promoters urged him to turn pro. When he biked throughout Europe, he could cover ninety miles in eight hours, and when he hiked the High Sierra, it was at a steady three miles an hour.

Thanks to his years studying at the University of Oxford in England, Hubble affected a slight British accent that some found entrancing, others not. He ordered all his suits from a British tailor and often wore a black cape and used a cane. He didn't crack jokes or laugh much. Dignified, perhaps arrogant, he wrote to his former Oxford classmates that he was busy "toying with such minor matters as the structure of the universe."

Stars were always Hubble's true love. For his eighth birthday, he didn't want a party; he asked instead to stay up all night and watch the stars through a telescope his grandfather had built. He wanted to study astronomy—first as a scholarship student at the University of Chicago and later at Oxford—but his overbearing father insisted he get a law degree.

There is no evidence that Hubble ever practiced law. He became a popular teacher of high school Spanish, and then, when his father died, resumed his starry studies. His reputation as an astronomer began to soar. War intervened, and he enlisted in the U.S. Army to serve in World War I, rising to the rank of major. While he fought in combat, his right elbow was injured, and it never fully healed.

The Mount Wilson Observatory in Southern California didn't care. It wanted Hubble so badly that it held a position open for him until after the war. Within a few years he was making major discoveries, and he worked at the observatory for the rest of his life.

Jazzed to be using the brand-new one-hundred-inch Hooker Telescope, then the most powerful on earth, Hubble stared deep into space each night. Most scientists agreed that the beautiful Milky Way galaxy made up the entire universe. Hubble, however, discovered that the Milky Way is just one of millions of galaxies. The universe was much larger than anyone thought. And, to top it all off, it was expanding.

Hubble did all his mind-blowing work in the unheated bunker atop the chilly peak of Mount Wilson. On the coldest nights his eyelashes would freeze to the eyepiece of the telescope, and his fingers and toes would go numb. To while away the hours between discoveries, he played solitaire, reconstructed old poems and beloved cowboy songs in his head, or broke for a midnight "lunch" of crackers and cocoa. Sometimes he was joined by deer, and once by a mountain lion that darted back into the forest.

Though Hubble relied on the data of astronomer Henrietta Swan Leavitt, among others, women were not allowed to use the instruments at Mount Wilson or even enter the living quarters. Indeed, he once said, "The great body of women could be divided into two classes, parasites and satellites."

At age thirty-four he found one he liked—Grace, an expert horsewoman and graduate of Stanford University—and gave her a book of romantic poems by Percy Bysshe Shelley. He spent evenings wooing her by reading aloud by the fireplace, often

with her parents there. She never met his parents, nor his brothers or sisters. After their marriage, she kept detailed journals of their hectic social life and apparently didn't mind that he read and corrected them for accuracy.

They built their dream house in San Marino, modeling it after a palace they'd seen in Florence. The property happened to be on an earthquake fault, which Hubble found amusing. Every Sunday they strolled the lush grounds of the Huntington Library. His spacious office had stained-glass windows and displayed a tooth from the saber-toothed tiger skeleton that had been found in the nearby La Brea Tar Pits. Their cat, named for astronomer Nicholas Copernicus, slept at the foot of their bed at night and all over the papers in Hubble's office during the day. When his owners were out of town, Copernicus joined the family's dogs at the Dude Ranch for Dogs.

Though he served in both world wars, Hubble came to be antiwar: "Warfare with the new weapons will be the ruin of civilization as we know it. . . . We are part of an organic whole, members of one body."

All the Hollywood stars of the day, as well as bigwigs from around the world, streamed to see the observatory and to have lunch with the Hubbles on Woodstock Road. Albert Einstein, moviemaker Walt Disney, and their favorite actor, Charlie Chaplin, fawned over them, and Hubble was once introduced at the the Oscar ceremonies by director Frank Capra as the world's greatest living astronomer.

Hubble often partied with his neighbors over glasses of French wine, sherry, or gin. He had a habit of flipping through the *Encyclopedia Britannica* before dinner, then stumping his guests with questions he would answer by triumphantly pulling out the appropriate volume. He compulsively smoked a pipe and could blow perfect smoke rings. He loved fly-fishing, especially at the White River in Colorado. Worried about smog in Los Angeles—and its effect on stargazing—he was head of the Pure Air Council of Southern California. Though he'd taught Sunday school classes at his Baptist church as a youth, he rarely spoke of religion as an adult. Two of his favorite words were "adventure" and "dream."

A notoriously bad driver, Hubble died of a stroke at age sixty-three in his car while Grace was driving him home from an errand. There was no funeral, and his ashes were buried in a secret location.

EXTRA CREDIT

Much to his frustration, Hubble never won the Nobel Prize—and not for lack of trying. He even hired a publicity agent to make his case. Not until after his death did the Nobel committee decide that work in astronomy could qualify for the physics prize, but Hubble still can't win it; one has to be alive to be awarded a Nobel.

All sorts of things are named for Hubble, but the one that might have delighted him the most is the Hubble Space Telescope. A satellite observatory orbiting Earth for the purpose of mapping the universe, it was launched in 1990 and has led to one breakthrough observation after another.

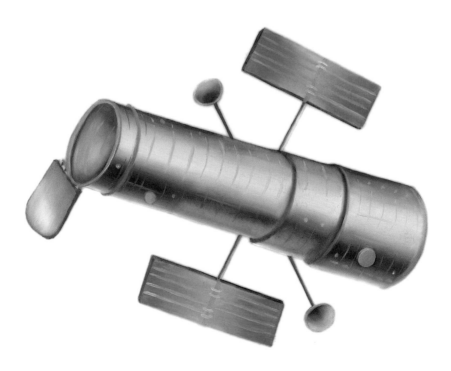

Watering Corn with Her Tears
Barbara McClintock

Born in Hartford, Connecticut, 1902
Died in Huntington, New York, 1992

American scientist famous for her work in genetics

For someone so devoted to corn, it was odd that Barbara McClintock didn't really enjoy eating it. Instead, she ate a chocolate a day—empty Godiva chocolates boxes would pile up. She also loved jelly beans and the scrumptious brownies she made with the black walnuts she collected on her walks.

Her love of corn wasn't about the taste—it was about the structure. And studying corn (specifically maize, or Indian corn) was a juicy enough subject to take up her entire life.

McClintock was an excellent student, but her mother feared that higher education would turn her daughter strange and "unmarriageable." Luckily, her father, a doctor, intervened. At Cornell University, when she wasn't playing banjo in a jazz group around town, she was taking her first courses in genes and genetics. McClintock was enchanted by this relatively new science, which built on the nineteenth-century work of Czech-German scientist Gregor Mendel. She sometimes dated classmates in her first years, but then seemed to decide she was too independent for relationships. Even as a baby, she had always preferred to be alone.

McClintock wanted to teach, but Cornell and other universities wouldn't hire a female professor. So many doors were closed to her after graduation that she almost gave up her dreams and became a weather forecaster. Finally, she got funding for research. But as a visiting researcher at the California Institute of Technology (which didn't hire a woman professor until decades later), she attracted so many stares at the faculty club—men would stop eating their lunch—that she murmured to her host, "What's wrong with me?"

When she joined the staff of the Carnegie Institution of Washington's genetics laboratory in Cold Spring Harbor, New York, she picked up a lack of "anti-female bias" and stayed. "I was just having a good time," McClintock said about her fifty years there. "I could hardly wait to get up in the morning."

Focusing on the relationship between plant reproduction and genetic mutation, she lovingly cared for a few hundred corn plants at a time, working twelve to sixteen hours every day of the week. Once, after a flood, she replanted her babies at night, using the light from the headlights of her car because she couldn't wait until

morning. During a drought, she built a system of pipes to get water to the plants; exhausted from standing in the sun, she cried, her tears combining with the water. To scare off the corn-eating raccoons when they were especially active, she would spend the night in a sleeping bag in the cornfields. Otherwise she slept across the street in an unheated garage converted into a sparsely furnished apartment; in the mornings she had to dart across a busy highway to get to work at the lab.

To get more corn samples to study, McClintock began journeying to South and Central America. She watched Spanish-language TV shows to become more fluent. She also taught maize genetics to graduate students. She was apparently tough— "Everyone was scared of her," said one student. One man was so frightened of McClintock that he would slip out the back door of the classroom whenever she entered the front.

After studying corn for so many years, McClintock could look at it through a

microscope and see structures no one else could: namely, how chromosomes formed the building blocks of cells. It was the birth of modern molecular genetics, with its astounding discoveries—about heredity, how and why traits are passed down through generations, how mutations can cause diseases that can then be diagnosed and treated. But she was so far ahead of her time that other scientists didn't catch on at first. Or perhaps they considered her subject—corn—too silly, and McClintock herself too solitary.

Undiscouraged, she never stopped her research. An important biologist called her "an old bag," but McClintock began racking up prestigious awards, including the first "genius grant" from the MacArthur Foundation, which gave her $60,000 a year for life. One morning in 1983, she was listening to the radio in her apartment when she heard that she'd just won the Nobel Prize in Physiology or Medicine. (She didn't own a phone, so the award committee couldn't call to tell her.)

"I do not like publicity," said McClintock in response to a book published about her. In public she started wearing a Groucho Marx disguise: plastic nose, glasses, and mustache.

Despite her intensity, she had a good sense of humor, a pleasant belly laugh, and a favorite color—red, which she chose for kitchen bowls, utensils, and appliances. She sometimes ate her meals in the lab's dining room with friends, or else heated food up on a hot plate right in the lab. She liked to take visitors for nature walks, and even expert biologists could learn something new from her. She befriended her neighbors' young children, who helped her pick walnuts for the brownies.

But she always lived and worked alone, even changing her own tires on her Model A Ford. She was as neat with her clothing as her data; she always wore tan pants or ironed jeans and a crisp white shirt. In her closet the hangers all faced the same direction and didn't touch. She considered packing for a trip a dreadful chore: "a great clothes burden for decorating the body."

She smoked, but otherwise lived healthily. She played tennis every day, sometimes went running and swimming, and in her eighties took up aerobic dancing.

After snowstorms she shoveled her own sidewalk and driveway. At the dentist, she turned down painkillers, claiming that she could conquer pain with her mind. Her mind was more open than most scientists' on her shelves were books about acupuncture, UFOs, ESP, and Buddhism.

She worked until ninety years of age, dying of natural causes.

EXTRA CREDIT

⌒ McClintock's discovery of transposable genes, known as "jumping genes," led to many medical breakthroughs and is the basis for today's cutting-edge research in genetic engineering.

⌒ As a young man, future Nobel Prize winner James D. Watson played baseball in a field next to McClintock's cornfield; he recalled her being irate when the ball flew into her turf. Not holding a grudge, he later proclaimed her one of "the three M's," the three most important figures in the history of genetics; the other two were American Thomas Hunt Morgan and Gregor Mendel.

"Computers Were More Fun"

Grace Murray Hopper

Born in New York City, 1906
Died in Arlington, Virginia, 1992

American pioneer of computer science

When Grace Murray Hopper was seven, she took her alarm clock apart to see how it worked. Her parents were impressed—until she took apart seven more. They limited her to dismantling one clock at a time, but they fully supported her education.

In college she played basketball, studied math and physics, and earned her doctorate (for a paper called "New Types of Irreducibility Criteria"). She became a popular math professor at Vassar College for women.

With ancestors who had served in the American Revolution, Hopper was anxious to serve during World War II. She was considered too old (at thirty-four) and underweight (at 105 pounds), but she persisted until she was accepted by the Naval Reserve.

On her first day at the Bureau of Ordnance Computation Project, armed guards escorted her to a room at Harvard University. They led her to their monstrous secret weapon. Called the Automatic Sequence Controlled Calculator, it was fifty feet long, eight feet high, and weighed 9,445 pounds. Hopper's boss said, "There's the machine. Compute the coefficients of the arc tangent series by next Thursday."

"All I could do was look at it," Hopper said later. It was the world's first computer (though the word wouldn't be used for several more years), and Hopper became one of its first programmers. She described herself as "thoroughly scared," but she got right to work.

On call twenty-four hours a day, she slept at her desk, used humor and patience to deal with overbearing men, and wrote the first computer operation manual (561 pages). "Grace was a good man!" said one boss. She dealt with the stress of her job by smoking and drinking alcohol (she was once arrested for disorderly conduct).

After the war, she divorced her husband, an English professor who had supported her ambitions. She didn't return to teaching because "computers were more fun." In the growing computer industry, she gave speeches about all that computers could do and tried to attract more women to the field. Her greatest feat was laying the foundation for COBOL (COmmon Business-Oriented Language), the most widely used programming language in the world.

Hopper was named the first "Computer Science Man of the Year" by a professional association and received a slew of other awards. Advancing to the rank of rear admiral, she never really retired from the navy. She died at age eighty-five.

The sentence Hopper had hated most was "But we've always done it this way."

Imagining Surf

Rachel Carson

Born in Springdale, Pennsylvania, 1907
Died in Silver Spring, Maryland, 1964

*American marine biologist considered
the founder of environmental science*

Rachel Carson's love of writing started at age eleven, when she sold her first animal story to a magazine. Her passion for biology began in college, when a class reawakened the sense of wonder she'd felt as a child. Her mother had taken her exploring every day around their sixty-five-acre farm, and Carson always felt "happiest with wild birds and creatures as companions." Nature nourished her. Long before she saw an ocean, she would imagine how it looked and "what the surf sounded like."

In college, Carson considered herself a poet and collected rejection slips from just about every magazine published. She was later world-famous for her clear, jargon-free writing, though her first major science paper was called "The Development of the Pronephros During the Embryonic and Early Larval Life of the Catfish."

With few jobs for women in science, Carson cleverly combined her passions for nature and writing when she joined the U.S. Fish and Wildlife Service. For sixteen years she worked her way up to becoming an aquatic biologist and the department's star writer. Coworkers remembered the sound of her high heels rapidly approaching and departing. She hated being indoors but needed the security of a job to support her mother and extended family.

Finally, when Carson was forty-four, her book *The Sea Around Us* made her financially secure, though she lost twenty pounds during the turmoil of its success and her unexpected fame. The money let her quit her day job, buy a new Oldsmobile, and take care of her health, which had never been strong. It also allowed her to build her dream house, called Silverledges, directly over the tide pools on the Maine coast. Later, she even bought a mink coat, something she'd always craved despite her usual anti-materialism.

"No time," she said when asked why she never married. It was more fun to explore the "undaunted efforts of the adventurous mind." She always saw herself as a biologist, not a crusader. She'd wear holes in her pants while sitting on barnacle-encrusted rocks to observe anemones and crabs, or stay in icy water so long she'd go numb and have to be carried ashore. Her mother typed her manuscripts, made their meals (Carson hated to cook), and acted as her daughter's biggest cheerleader.

Carson was a total cat person, and for almost twenty years she lived with a family of cats that often sprawled on the table while she wrote. Extremely private and deeply spiritual, she saw zero conflict between science and religion; her books came

to be quoted in many sermons. Her closest friendship was with a neighbor, Dorothy; the two women shared an interest in Leonard Bernstein's music and in preserving the wilderness behind their homes.

It took four years for Carson to marshal her facts for *Silent Spring,* an attention-grabbing book about the effect of certain pesticides on nature. Opponents attacked it as science fiction akin to *The Twilight Zone,* as the work of a "hysterical woman" or a "spinster" oddly concerned with the health of future generations, and as unpatriotic for not supporting American science. But the runaway bestseller woke people up—leading to a nationwide ban on DDT and other pesticides, inspiring the creation of the Environmental Protection Agency, and encouraging millions to get passionate about protecting human health and the environment.

Eighteen months after its publication, Carson died of breast cancer at age fifty-six. In one of her last letters to Dorothy, she wrote, "Not long ago I sat late in my study and played Beethoven, and achieved a feeling of real peace and even happiness."

"A Dear Old Friend"
Chien-Shiung Wu

BORN IN SHANGHAI, CHINA, 1912
DIED IN NEW YORK CITY, 1997

Chinese-American physicist sometimes called the First Lady of Physics

"Ignore the obstacles and keep walking ahead," Chien-Shiung Wu's father said. In China at the time, some girls still had their feet painfully bound and were thus unable to walk, and none went to school. Wu's father founded a girls' school so his daughter could have an education, which then took her away from home and family.

At Nanjing University, professors bragged about their best student, and it was always the same person—Wu. At twenty-four, she took the long steamship voyage alone to study in the United States, planning to return to help China modernize. Horrified by the choices in the cafeteria at the University of California at Berkeley, she located a Chinese caterer who charged her twenty-five cents to eat leftovers.

Once she forgot to put the cap back on a mercury bottle, and her professor left her a note: "The vapor is poisonous. Do you want to see your grandchildren?" Seldom that careless, she was so dedicated that she often stayed at the lab until three or four a.m.

After difficulty finding a teaching position worthy of her, she made it to Columbia University. She spent thirty-six years there as a physics professor with a lab of her own. She pushed students hard, especially girls: "It is shameful that there are so few women in science." Some grumbled, calling her "Dragon Lady," and claimed that she was "never satisfied."

Wu married another physicist, Luke Chia-Liu Yuan, and had a son who became a physicist. She ordered her clothes from China or Taiwan, and always preferred Chinese food, tracking down favorite chefs whenever they changed restaurants.

She was best known for her elegant experiments and wise advice, consistently gaining respect from male physicists. When anyone had questions, they were told: "Ask Miss Wu." Her specialty became beta decay, an area of nuclear physics that after years of study felt to her like "a dear old friend." Wanting to be the first to solve a certain problem, she spent six months sleeping just four hours a night and taking fifteen-minute lunch breaks; she let her husband go on their twentieth-anniversary cruise alone.

Her experiments overturned a basic rule in physics: the tricky "law of conservation of parity," which specifies that elementary particles and their mirror images should behave identically. Wu discovered that certain "weak" nuclear interactions violate this law. She celebrated the discovery by drinking champagne from tiny paper cups with her co-workers. The two male physicists who used her experiments won the 1957 Nobel Prize in Physics. Wu won nearly every other science prize and became the first living scientist to have an asteroid named after her.

By the time she was finally able to return to China in 1973, all her family members there were dead. Wu died after a stroke at the age of eighty-four.

"Two People Are Better Than One"

James D. Watson and Francis Crick

BORN IN CHICAGO, ILLINOIS, 1928 (WATSON)

BORN IN NORTHAMPTON, ENGLAND, 1916;
DIED IN SAN DIEGO, CALIFORNIA, 2004 (CRICK)

American and British molecular biologists, discoverers of the structure of DNA

One day in 1953, two scientists walked into the Eagle, a dark pub in Cambridge, England. Over glasses of beer they announced to the lunchtime crowd that they had just discovered the secret of life. Scientist Francis Crick's wife, an artist named Odile, didn't believe him: "You were always coming home and saying things like that, so naturally I thought nothing of it." That didn't stop Odile from going out to buy champagne and chilling it in their bathtub for one of their famous parties that night.

The other scientist, James D. Watson, described his mood as "sheer ecstasy." That morning, within the Cavendish Laboratory at the University of Cambridge, he and Crick had figured out the structure of deoxyribonucleic acid, or DNA. As Crick told his twelve-year-old son, it was "the basic copying mechanism by which life comes from life." Odile, who usually drew nudes, later sketched the structure as a spiraling staircase or a twisting ladder. This structure, that of a "double helix" that can "unzip" to make copies of itself, confirmed the theory that DNA carries life's hereditary information. Its discovery ultimately won Crick and Watson the 1962 Nobel Prize in Medicine. Each insisted he could not have done it without the other.

Watson was American, twenty-four at the time of the discovery, and freely admitted that "almost everything I ever did, even as a scientist, was in the hope of meeting a pretty girl." Unathletic, shy, and unpopular as a child, he had been bullied and beaten up. At fourteen he became one of radio's high-IQ "Quiz Kids" in a show produced by one of his neighbors. An avid bird watcher, he used his quiz-show winnings to buy a better pair of binoculars. The next year he was admitted to the University of Chicago after only two years of high school.

Crick was British and thirty-six, married with children, off to a late start after developing magnetic mines for naval warfare and swearing he'd never work on weapons again. He freely admitted he was "a rather sloppy thinker" who did best with a partner: "Two people are better than one. Otherwise you get in a rut."

Watson called Crick "no doubt the brightest person I have ever known. . . . He never stops talking or thinking." Yet a colleague complained that Crick's "method of

working was to talk loudly all the time," and numerous people complained about his high-pitched laugh.

Watson and Crick had read the same book—*What Is Life? The Physical Aspect of the Living Cell,* by Austrian physicist Erwin Schrödinger—at almost exactly the same time. Once they met at the University of Cambridge, they realized that they shared an interest in winning the race to discover the secrets of DNA. For almost two years before their breakthrough, they talked nonstop during walks along the river and over lunches at the pub and delicious dinners cooked by Odile.

At the Nobel ceremony, Crick danced with his eleven-year-old daughter, while Watson later said, "I did not belong on a dance floor." He viewed the Nobel as a way to get more dates. "I like women, but they don't seem to like me," he mourned.

One of the few times one was jealous of the other was when Watson, though not normally considered stylish, appeared in glamorous *Vogue* magazine. He was featured in the back-to-school issue as one of eighteen talented young people. Coincidentally (and surprisingly), *Vogue* was Crick's favorite magazine, and he resented the attention.

Crick moved on to swim in the heated pools of Southern California, doing brain research and cultivating his privacy. He printed up a card declining seventeen specific requests, from giving autographs to getting honorary degrees. An outspoken atheist, he refused to attend religious ceremonies, though he didn't mind going if there was a party afterward. At Crick's fiftieth birthday party, Watson arranged for a bikini-clad woman named Fifi to jump out of the cake. In his last book, Crick speculated about aliens seeding the universe with life forms. He died of colon cancer at age eighty-eight.

As for Watson, a professor once described him as "the most unpleasant human being I had ever met," a man who "radiated contempt in all directions." Easily bored, Watson often asked rude questions or opened a book when others were speaking. But he went on to become a public figure, head of the Cold Spring Harbor Laboratory in New York, using his celebrity to raise funds for it: "I really like rich people."

Also an atheist, he was known to make politically incorrect outbursts. He cultivated his geeky image, sometimes preparing for a meeting by untying his tennis shoes, messing up his hair, and dusting chalk on his suit. He wrote best-selling books about himself, spicing them with gossip, which he adored.

At thirty-nine, he finally "found the needed beautiful girl" and married Elizabeth, a college sophomore from Radcliffe; they had two sons. Wealthy neighbors helped him turn his lab into a world-renowned center for research on cancer, Alzheimer's disease, and, after one son developed schizophrenia, mental illness. "I think science can improve human life," Watson always maintained. After one too many controversial remarks, he announced his retirement in 2007.

That same year, Watson became the second person to have his personal gene sequence made known online. It was appropriate, because he'd helped found the Human Genome Project, mapping all the genes of the human genome, the code for a person's heredity information.

EXTRA CREDIT

◟◞ Crick and Watson shared their Nobel Prize with New Zealand biologist Maurice Wilkins, and all three were indebted to the work of Rosalind Franklin, a British biophysicist. Working in a mostly male field at a time when women weren't even allowed in the faculty coffee room, Franklin had no one to bond with and worked alone. She died of cancer in 1958, at thirty-seven, and Nobel Prizes aren't given posthumously; Crick estimated she had been only months or weeks behind them in making their great discovery.

◟◞ As excited as scientists were about DNA, it was not until the 1980s that the concept of DNA became familiar to the public. By that time it had become key evidence in identifying criminals in notorious trials and scandals.

Wilkins

Franklin

From Waitress to World Expert

Jane Goodall

Born in London, England, 1934

Pioneering English ethologist known for findings in chimpanzee behavior

"I was madly in love with the Lord of the Jungle," Jane Goodall once confessed about herself as a girl, little knowing how many "Me, Tarzan—you, Jane" jokes she would hear later.

From an early age she had a love for animal books and animals themselves, whether toy or real, wild or tame. Her fiercest desire became to leave London and see wild animals in Africa. With little money, she took a roundabout way, fending off marriage proposals to earn money instead. She typed fifty-one words a minute as a secretary (her secretarial school called her a "clever girl, but rather smug"). Mastering the art of carrying up to thirteen dinner plates without dropping any, she was a waitress, working herself "to the bone" until she finally earned the fare to visit a school friend in Kenya.

Age twenty-three on this first trip to Africa, she immediately felt at home in her unpredictable new surroundings. To a friend she wrote, "Out here I am no longer mad—because everyone is mad." Within weeks, she met Louis Leakey, the famous archaeologist, who guided her career even after she made it clear she wasn't romantically interested in him. She called him FFF, her Fairy Foster Father.

At Gombe Stream National Park in Tanzania, Goodall showed extraordinary

patience with chimpanzees, taking notes while watching them from a distance with binoculars. She would leave camp while it was still dark, climbing through thick brush. With a mild case of a disorder that made it difficult for her to recognize faces and places, she sometimes got lost. She occasionally stayed out overnight, or hiked nude in the rainy season, toting her clothes in a plastic bag to keep them dry.

But Goodall later looked back on this time as "paradise . . . magic." At first the chimps fled whenever they saw her, but gradually they allowed her to come closer. One day, she wrote about a favorite: "David Greybeard has—yes—he has TAKEN BANANAS FROM MY HAND."

She hurried back to England to get proper credentials, earning her doctorate in ethology (the comparative study of animal behavior) from the University of Cambridge. Thousands and thousands of pages of chimp notes later, she became famous as the world's expert on chimpanzee behavior. She corrected many misunderstandings about primates and revealed the social similarities between chimps and humans, both good and bad.

She married a Dutch wildlife photographer; their wedding cake was topped with a model of Greybeard, and "our conversation is mostly—chimp—chimp—and more chimp." Their son, known as "Grub," found the chimps scary, but Goodall later rejoiced that her grandson was fascinated. After divorcing, she married the director of Tanzania's national parks, who died five years into their marriage.

Since 1986, saddened by threats to chimp survival, she has devoted her life to making people aware of their endangerment. As much as she misses the chimps, she travels about three hundred days per year to visit schools and make speeches about protecting animals and the environment, rarely staying more than two nights in each place. She always carries a stuffed chimp, Mr. H., as an icebreaker. Though she can raise more than two million dollars a year for her cause, she lives simply and travels lightly, always serene and down to earth, still with unusual stamina. Very spiritual, she sees no conflict between religion and science.

Whenever she is asked "What's the secret of your youth?" she replies, "There's so much to do."

FOR FURTHER READING

Al-Khalili, Jim. *The House of Wisdom: How Arabic Science Saved Ancient Knowledge and Gave Us the Renaissance.* New York: Penguin, 2011.

Beyer, Kurt W. *Grace Hopper and the Invention of the Information Age.* Cambridge, Massachusetts: MIT Press, 2009.

Bolden, Tonya. *George Washington Carver.* New York: Abrams, 2008.

Browne, Janet. *Charles Darwin, Volume 1* (1995) and *Volume 2* (2002). New York: Knopf.

Christianson, Gale E. *Edwin Hubble: Mariner of the Nebulae.* New York: Farrar, Straus and Giroux, 1995.

Comfort, Nathaniel C. *The Tangled Field: Barbara McClintock's Search for the Patterns of Genetic Control.* Cambridge, Massachusetts: Harvard University Press, 2001.

Cooperman, Stephanie H. *Chien-Shiung Wu: Pioneering Physicist and Atomic Researcher.* New York: Rosen, 2004.

Debré, Patrice. *Louis Pasteur.* Baltimore, Maryland: Johns Hopkins University Press, 1998.

Gleick, James. *Isaac Newton.* New York: Pantheon, 2003.

Goldsmith, Barbara. *Obsessive Genius: The Inner World of Marie Curie.* New York: Norton, 2005.

Greene, Meg. *Jane Goodall: A Biography.* Amherst, New York: Prometheus, 2008.

Heilbron, J. L. *Galileo.* New York: Oxford University Press, 2010.

Isaacson, Walter. *Einstein: His Life and Universe.* New York: Simon & Schuster, 2007.

Lemonick, Michael D. *The Georgian Star: How William and Caroline Herschel Revolutionized Our Understanding of the Cosmos.* New York: Norton, 2009.

Lytle, Mark Hamilton. *The Gentle Subversive: Rachel Carson, Silent Spring, and the Rise of the Environmental Movement.* New York: Oxford University Press, 2007.

McElheny, Victor K. *Watson & DNA: Making a Scientific Revolution.* New York: Basic Books, 2004.

Ridley, Matt. *Francis Crick: Discoverer of the Genetic Code.* New York: HarperCollins, 2006.

Temple, Robert. *The Genius of China: 3,000 Years of Science, Discovery, and Invention.* New York: Simon & Schuster, 1986.

Todes, Daniel P. *Pavlov's Physiology Factory: Experiment, Interpretation, Laboratory Enterprise.* Baltimore, Maryland: Johns Hopkins University Press, 2002.